20 Christmas Carols
For Solo Oboe
Book 2

Michael Shaw

Music Arrangements. All Christmas Carol arrangements in this book by **Michael Shaw Copyright © 2015**

ISBN: 1517159326
ISBN-13: 978-1517159320

www.mikesmusicroom.co.uk

Contents

Introduction

The Christmas sheet music in this book has been arranged for easy solo Oboe.

You can also play together in a duet or ensemble with other instruments with a book for that instrument. To get a book for an instrument other than your own, choose from the 20 Christmas Carols Series Book 2. All arrangements are the same and keys are adjusted for B flat, E flat, F and C instruments so everything sounds correct. Instruments in this series include Tenor Saxophone, Clarinet, French Horn, Trumpet, Flute, Trombone and Oboe. Please check out my author page on Amazon to view these books.

Author Page US
amazon.com/Michael-Shaw/e/B00FNVFJGQ/

Author Page UK
amazon.co.uk/Michael-Shaw/e/B00FNVFJGQ/

Christians Awake Salute The Happy Morn

Arr. Michael Shaw

Oboe

Traditional

Oboe

Ob.

Ob.

Ob.

Ob.

Ob.

Come, All Ye Shepherds

Arr. Michael Shaw

Oboe

Traditional

Coventry Carol

Arr. Michael Shaw

Oboe

Traditional

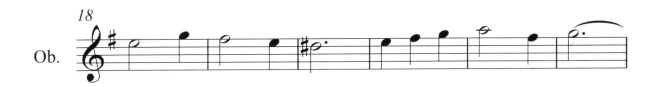

The Huron Carol
Oboe

Arr. Michael Shaw

Traditional

The Wassail Song

Arr. Michael Shaw

Oboe

Traditional

I Heard The Bells On Christmas Day

Arr. Michael Shaw

Oboe

John Baptiste Calkin

The Wexford Carol

Arr. Michael Shaw

Oboe

Traditional Irish

Oboe

poco rall.

See Amid The Winter's Snow

Arr. Michael Shaw

Oboe

John Goss

Oboe

9

In The Bleak Midwinter

Arr. Michael Shaw

Oboe

Gustav Holst

Oboe

Ob.

Ob.

Ob.

Ob.

Angels We Have Heard On High

Arr. Michael Shaw

Oboe

Traditional

O Come O Come Emmanuel

Arr. Michael Shaw

Oboe

15th Century French

O Little Town Of Bethlehem

Arr. Michael Shaw

Oboe

Traditional

Gather Around The Christmas Tree

Arr. Michael Shaw

Oboe

Traditional

Oboe

4

Ob.

8

Ob.

12

Ob.

15

Ob.

15

O Holy Night

Arr. Michael Shaw

Oboe

Adolphe Adam

Oboe

6

Ob.

12

Ob.

16

Ob.

20

Ob.

The Gloucestershire Wassail

Arr. Michael Shaw

Oboe

Traditional

Oboe

It Came Upon The Midnight Clear

Arr. Michael Shaw

Oboe

Traditional

Oboe

Ob.

Ob.

Ob.

Ob.

Ob.

Good Christian Men Rejoice

Arr. Michael Shaw

Oboe

Traditional

Angels From The Realms Of Glory

Arr. Michael Shaw

Oboe

Henry Smart

Go Tell It On The Mountain

Arr. Michael Shaw

Oboe

Traditional

Unto Us A Boy Is Born

Arr. Michael Shaw

Oboe

Traditional

About the Author

Mike works as a professional musician and keyboard music teacher. Mike has been teaching piano, electronic keyboard and electric organ for over thirty years and as a keyboard player worked in many night clubs and entertainment venues.

Mike has also branched out in to composing music and has written and recorded many new royalty free tracks which are used worldwide in TV, film and internet media applications. Mike is also proud of the fact that many of his students have gone on to be musicians, composers and teachers in their own right.

You can connect with Mike at:

Facebook
facebook.com/keyboardsheetmusic

Soundcloud
soundcloud.com/audiomichaeld

YouTube
youtube.com/user/pianolessonsguru

I hope this book has helped you with your music, if you have received value from it in any way, then I'd like to ask you for a favour: would you be kind enough to leave a review for this book on Amazon? It'd be greatly appreciated!

Thank You
Michael Shaw

Made in the USA
Las Vegas, NV
23 October 2021